Matthew James

Let Me Put My POEMS IN YOU

Love! Sex! Comedy! Prejudice?

VANCOUVER:
ENGAGE BOOKS LIMITED
2015

this

book

is

dedicated

to

beautiful

women

everywhere

CONTENTS

ODE TO BEER

Oh to beer, sweet sudsy beer
Oh how it is that I revere
Your flavours like a rainbow are
So many choices at the bar
Oh how am I to choose but one
No that would not be too much fun
You've been with me through thick and thin
Through ups and downs, the vomit bin
Oh loyal beer sweet nectar true
It's liquid bread it's good for you

PETER PIPER, THAT DIRTY BUGGER

Peter Piper piped his peter in between her

ROCK STAR

To be a rock star, I suppose
Is to have your way with thus and those
To lay with whom you choose to lay
And stray with whom you choose to stray

To be a rock star, I surmise
Means getting her right in the eyes
With loving juice she squeezed by hand
Or mouth or nether region land

MAN DEFINED

What meanest it to be a man
To have a wang and be a fan
Of sport, but firstly of woman
Of what the Chinese call "Poon Tang"

To be a man I have to say
Means that you'll seldom get your way
And that you'll always have to stay
Faithful or else you'll have to pay

ODE TO THE EXOTIC DANCER

Oh to the exotic dancer
What would life be were you not to answer
Your cue from the DJ to get on stage
The clientele would surely rage
And bachelor parties would be no longer
My that day would be quite somber
Oh to the exotic dancer
Bravo

SEA LOVERS

I do not refrain
Nor do I restrain
Myself at the beach
Nothing's out of reach

There are two of you
And I want to do
Both of you right hear
Right under the pier

Let's make it happen
Aside with caution
Take your bikinis
Off here in the seas

Does it not feel right?
Here just out of sight
Our love fest of three
Lovers in the sea

NEGLECT

Roses are red, violets are blue
The same color as my manhood
When you neglect me for days
And I'm too lazy to take matters into my own hands

DIRTY DUCK

How come ducks are always in pairs?
Have you ever noticed that, how they're always in pairs?
You never see a duck by itself
It's always with a partner
I've heard they mate for life but how do you know for sure?
That crazy mallard could have
A different lady duck with him every time you see him
How would you know the difference?
I mean they're ducks,
You're telling me you can tell the difference between them?
I don't think so
Therefore I'm throwing this out there
Ducks are players
They bounce from mate to mate
Like Henry the eight went through wives
So the next time you see a duck don't say
Hey, did you know that ducks mate for life?
No, instead say, Hey there goes that little player

MAKE IT WITH YOU

When the day is gray
And you're lazing away
You've got nothing to do
And you just want to screw
Go get your lady
And say hey baby
I want to make it with you

NANTUCKET

There once was a man from Nantucket
Who went to the beach with a bucket
He filled it with sand
His castle was grand
You thought I was going to say fuck it

IT'S NOT THE LIGHTING

There once was a man from Surrey
Who wished to get busy in a hurry
He got in his car
And went to the bar
When seen all the women did scurry

BEWARE THE CAMERA PHONE

When the bright light of the full moon shines upon the Earth
And illuminates that dark alley for all to see
Don't be the guy going at it with a he/she
People have cameras on their phones nowadays
And they won't hesitate to put that disgusting act on the internet

IN DENIAL

"Beauty is in the eye of the beholder"
He said with conviction
Standing in an art gallery
Speaking with a stranger
When from around the corner
Appeared the man's wife
Woof!

SOME PEOPLE HAVE REALLY SHITTY JOBS

I saw a bumper sticker the other day
It said "the worst day fishing is better than the best day working"
I had to think to myself, "where does this guy work?"
I mean I've been fishing before
And I've been to work plenty
I've been fishing when it was very cold
When the rain was falling from the sky,
With the fury of a woman scorned
When the gusting winds had stirred up such big ocean swells
That vomiting took the place of fishing
Where if someone at that very moment gave me a loaded gun
There may not have been much debate,
Over pulling the trigger to end the suffering
This brings me back to my initial thought
If the worst day fishing is truly better than this man's job
What does he do for a living?
Are the products that are not tested on animals tested on him instead?
Do they test out new proctology equipment on him?
What is it this man does for a living?
I would like to know

SUPERMAN

Did you ever wonder why
Nobody ever recognized Superman
When he was dressed as Clark Kent?
I always did
All he did was replace the spandex suit with a proper suit
Part his hair on the other side of his head
And put a pair of glasses on his face
How could nobody have ever recognized him?
I guess people are just retarded

DESTINED FOR DETAINMENT

Out of wedlock the baby came
Into the world without a name
His mother but a lowly teen
His father absent from the scene

He will grow up without a dad
And mother who'd wish she never had
Him, no chance the boy doth have
In this cruel world where many have

To prison he will surely go
Be forced to take and forced to blow
He'll turn into an angry man
To be released out of the can

And when he's back out on the street
Back to the crime he will retreat

PHYSICAL LOVE

Hey baby, let us make love
Like two wild animals
Whom after a hard day of hunting
Have the need for a feast
But not the eating kind of feast
No, but the loving kind

I want to put my baby makers
Into your baby factory
They're good hard workers
And trust me, you'll enjoy the introduction
So why don't you let me give you what I know you want
Because baby, I want to show my love to you, physically

RING GIRLS

There are many different professions
In this diverse World we live in
But not all of them are common place
So I wonder how you get into them

Like ring girls at fight events
Who walk around the ring each round
Holding a large cardboard number
High up over their heads

How did they get into this
Silliest of professions?
Was it a lifetime goal of theirs
Or was it stumbled into?

To walk around the ring half naked
In between the rounds
Is such an odd job
But I am still thankful for them

For what would fight night really be
Without scantily clad women
Walking all around the ring
In sneakers and bikinis

So thank you ring girls everywhere
I love what you are doing
While your job is unusual
What would we do without you?

SUCKERS WE ARE

Work is for us suckers
And suckers we are
We wake everyday to the sound of alarm
Forced to rise well before we please
We shave and shower and maybe we eat
And wonder from the house like a zombie
Leaving always in a hurry
We rush to work for no good reason
Other than to not be late
For there are always eyes upon us
They watch our every little move
And if we step just out of place
Those eyes are sure to catch us
Few are those who like their jobs
I am not of the few
But some day soon I hope to be
So sorry suckers

THE TAXMAN TAKETH

Taxes are the devil
I'm sure most would agree
They tax you on your income
They tax you on your tea

Taxes for your clothing
And taxes on your home
Sometimes there's tax on top of tax
Even on puppy's bone

The suffocating redundancy
Of paying all those bills
Has led me to an urgency
Of ending them with kills

Perhaps we hang the taxman
And torch his agency
For the only escape that we have
Is creating anarchy

DON'T JUDGE A BOOK BY ITS COVER

It was a day not unlike any other
On a street much like the street you may be driving on
Hey, pull over at least if you're driving while reading this
That's dangerous, I mean come on, have some sense
Sorry about that, anyway the street was not unordinary
But what was on the side of the street was
For a woman stood there, thumb in the air
Wearing nothing but a ten gallon hat
A man drove by and couldn't resist
For she was a beauty with very nice breasts
He pulled over and she came on over
She climbed in and they headed west
What happened next, I truly attest
And this information is third hand at best
But she pulled off her hat
And under it sat
A large black and silver revolver
She placed it to his head
Told him he was dead
If he didn't do as she told him
He did not disobey
Said he just wanted a lay
And asked how she could do this to him
"Don't judge a book by its cover" she said
Pulled back the trigger, gun still to his head
But it didn't go bang
Then the woman sang
"Happy birthday from the gang"

BEAUTY AT THE BAR

The party's on I'm at the bar
I'm feeling good cause I'm well lubed
And then I spot her from afar
She's dancing hard and looking good

I approach and take her hand
She puts my arms around her waist
We start to dance beside the band
I crush a drink too fast to taste

I'm rightly wasted, so is she
Into my pocket she does reach
Out comes my phone, she is a tease
She types and gives a little screech

Her number she did place on it
Then back to dancing on the floor
And then more drink I must admit
Until my memory was no more

A few days later I did call
So pleased she was to hear from me
Her face I just could not recall
Too many drinks had gone in me

My drunken memory seemed to perceive
That she was a beauty at the bar
But oh how liquor doth deceive
For when I pulled up in my car

She ran outside and frightened me
"That can't be her" I hoped and prayed
I looked away, afraid to see
But she climbed in my car and stayed

"Hello" she said, "how have you been?"
"Alright 'til now" I said in mind
For her very sight was quite obscene
It appeared I was in quite a bind

I remembered her to be a star
Obscenely drunk I must have been
For as I sat there in my car
No further off could I have been

I drove her to her favorite bar
She got out and walked to the door
And as I sat there in my car
I pinned the petal to the floor

The moral of the story told
You cannot trust your drunken eyes
For what they may in truth behold
A lady beast that's in disguise

VOULEZ VOUS COUCHER AVEC MOI?

A crazy night it was that eve
Ménage a trois? She asked of me
She was not alone but with a friend
Both beautiful and moral bent

Of course I could not disappoint
The girls alone and in my joint
They slowly pealed each other's clothes
I breathed in gently through my nose

Then one came 'ore and took my hand
I felt as such a lucky man
I followed her into the bed
What was that sound that's in my head?

A beeping that just wouldn't stop
Then I awoke, damn alarm clock

LADY KILLER

Raised to be a lady killer
He was known as quite the thriller
Seldom turned a lady down
Never made a lady frown

Until one day it hurt to pee
He had come down with some VD
The lady killer put to rest?
But surely ladies would protest

He took some drugs and he recovered
From then on out he used a rubber

MIND BLOWING

Hey baby, where you running off to?
Why don't you come have a seat right here
I've got some things I'd like to share with you
I'm going to put my poems in you
Figuratively that is
So loosen your pants and listen up
Because you're going to bust a gut

CRAZY BITCH

We had only just met earlier that night
But that didn't stop her from asking
She invited me back to her place
How could I resist
We walked in the door, the lights were all out
Taking me by the hand she pulled me upstairs
Honestly she didn't have to pull
I would have followed her anywhere
We got to the bedroom and I picked her up
I half tossed her onto the bed
Clothes off in seconds, no time was wasted
A wild woman she surely was
A few minutes later, downstairs
I heard the front door slam shut
It stopped me mid act
She told me it was her husband
There had been no previous mention of a husband
He was not expected home she said
Panicked, I jumped out of bed and gathered my clothes
I opened the window and with one foot outside
Turned to thank the lady for a lovely evening
She told me she loved me
Then I disappeared through the open window
Some women are just damn crazy

PANTY REMOVER

A lady of vim
So proper and prim
Turning her nose to the party

I bought her a gin
And with some chagrin
She drank it although she looked angry

My did she transform
She said she was warm
And then she just took off her panties

She performed a dance
The room she romanced
And really was acting quite sloppy

Little miss snob
Was rubbing his knob
Right there in front of the party

She gave a hiccup
And then she threw up
Proper miss snob had gone nasty

Gin it would seem
Can make you obscene
Even if you are quite snobby

So when you're in doubt
Just give gin a shout
And you'll be the life of the party

GOODBYE MY LOVE

A beautiful thing that she was
But I had to let her go
The circumstances called for it
I could no longer hold on to her

It hurt me dear, my emotions were clear
But none the less the time was up
I had to sell my motorcycle
Because life can sometimes be tough

ANTI DEPRESSANT?

When I'm feeling sad and lonely
And there's no one to console me
I always turn to liquor
Mother nature's fixer

So if you're feeling sad and blue
And you've got no one to turn to
Alcohol's the responsible choice
Drink it down and then rejoice

SEMANTICS

What some call the problem
Others call the cure
Who's right or who's wrong?
I can't be sure

It all boils down to be semantics
Let us agree to disagree
For it can cause some funny antics
Maybe we should just let it be

DON'T DROP THE SOAP

Drunk and disorderly
That's what they said
But we saw it differently
Bruised were our heads

Escorted to jail
And thrown in the tank
No one to post bail
The cell really stank

We got in a fight
Just after the game
For that is our plight
My hand was in pain

I had to go pee
Toilet right in the cell
But all around me
People looked straight from hell

I'd seen prison movies
So I held it in
To keep my virginity
In the sin bin

THE FAIRER SEX

What would life be
Without the fairer sex
It wouldn't be worth living
No not for me at least

There'd be no more bikinis
And no more lingerie
No flirting at the office
Or nightly escapades

If ladies were no longer
I'd end it all for sure
Life wouldn't be worth living
Without those sexy women

LOVE TRAIN

Riding on the love train
With many sexy ladies
Things are getting insane
It's time to make some babies

This is just like Eden
Or maybe like the Grotto
That tall hot blonde's from Sweden
It's time she learned my motto

Hey let's make a baby
I said to her with class
She said that I was crazy
Then slapped me on the ass

I like your sly demeanor
She told me with a smile
I took her to the bunker
Then we made love freestyle

Loving on the love train
With such a sexy Swede
I had to pop some champagne
To celebrate our deed

I'm classy like that

ODE TO THE YOGA PANT

Oh to the yoga pant
Your spandex fits so tightly
You're like a sculpting pushup bra
Except for ladies heinies

My neck gets sore when at the gym
For my head's on a swivel
There's sexy bottoms everywhere
It makes that dank place blissful

Whoever came up with these pants
He must have been a genius
For when I see that yoga ass
I feel it in my penis

ATHLETIC PROWESS

Oh to be a pro athlete
To make a living playing
Your salary like the lottery
And I'm not overstating

Revered by people everywhere
And idolized by children
Women throw themselves your way
And you have your way with them

For even the most unsightly of men
Can have a beautiful allotment
Of loose moral lady friends
And he can surely flaunt them

For many ladies love is not
To do with a connection
It is to do with wealth and fame
For which they'll show affection

Oh to be a pro athlete
Only in my dreams

THE HILLBILLY AND THE GOAT

Once upon a time down south
And I mean deep in country
There was a man who had a goat
Something about him was funny

His goat and he it seemed to be
Were never without the other
Always side by side you see
Or one behind the other

For this hillbilly had no teeth
His mother was his cousin
A disturbing love affair
He'd drummed up with said cousin

And one day she did break his heart
To the hills he went a running
He swore off women there and then
And guess who came a coming

A mountain goat, oh no
Crazy hillbilly

I LIKE YOU

Roses are red
Violets are blue
I like your vagina
And the rest of you too

BULLETPROOF

Ten feet tall and bullet proof
Is how she sees herself
She's only a mere couple pounds
Just like a puppy elf

That Chihuahua it seems to me
Has really got some gusto
She has been known to pick a fight
Just like a rabid dingo

Her limitations don't exist
At least not in her mind
That little dog thinks she's queen bitch
As long as I'm behind

ABSTRACT

Senseless acts of sexiness
Are always in your best interest
To appreciate and manipulate
To fornicate and copulate
If you don't know what I mean by this
That's ok, neither do I
For at this moment I am quite high

BAD GOVERNMENT

Cutbacks and layoffs
Government payoffs
Country in trouble
Turning to rubble
First world to third
While having a turd
Dropped right on your face
What a disgrace
We once were respected
Our country's defective
No respect for each other
How do we recover
So screw this place
Screw it right in the face
I'm out of here

MAN'S BEST FRIEND

If dog is truly man's best friend
What maketh that a woman
A dog is with you to the end
That's true of just some women

So happy your dog when you come home
Your woman may feel quite different
And if you throw him down a bone
It's more than just sufficient

So if a woman you doth find
Who treats you like your puppy
Then get a marriage license signed
Cause man you are quite lucky

NOT ONE FOR MOM

The sky was dark
The rain did plummet
A dreary day it was
The ides of April had come
Feeling stagnant, unmotivated
I sat without a thought
The phone did ring and I did answer
So happy that I had
It was a wrong number
But that didn't stop her
She spoke without a pause
Out from her mouth
Came such arousing filth
I put her on the speaker
I called my buddy to come listen
He could not believe his ears
"She just won't stop", I said to him
He said he had to meet her
"Where are you at" he said to her
She told him in an instant
"I'm off to find my one true love"
He said as he was leaving
The next day home my friend had come
"So how'd it go" I asked him
Unable to talk, he could barely walk
The world's biggest smile upon his face
Sometimes a lady's not a keeper
And you'd never show her to mom
But that doesn't mean you can't go see her
And have a world of fun

DEEP THOUGHTS

If life were a vacation
Would I still need a vacation
To escape the monotony
Of everyday life?

THE ULTIMATE PRIZE

You can call it a beaver
A love pump receiver
A box or a taco
A baby juice depot
A love nest or flower
The source of girl power
A peach or a pussy
A cooch or some nookie
A wild snatch to wrangle
The Bermuda triangle
But if you want to get it
You have to respect it
Few give it away
For merely some pay

CREATIVE MINDS ACROSS THE WORLD

It matters not where you roam
Or whereabouts you call home
Throughout the World everywhere
There is one thing we all share

It is not how we speak
Or when we go to sleep
And it isn't our culture
Nor our sense of humor

But there is this one thing
That is quite amazing
It shows creativity
And ingenuity

The ability to
Make alcoholic brew
From whatever is found
In the surrounding ground

From rice made to vodka
And cactus tequila
If it grows in the ground
It is alcohol bound

PORN FRIEND

Oh to the email forwarding buddy
That friend who forwards everything he comes across
And none more important than naked lady pictures
Oh where would we be without him?
Would we be forced to surf the internet for lady pictures ourselves?
Or would we be too lazy to even bother?
Thankfully that day will never come
For there appears to be no end in sight
To his chronic abuse of the forward button

THE OGRE

It was a dark and lonely night
And on that night I had a fright
Alone I sat there at the bar
She had been spotted from afar
A beast she was, oh quite obscene
I turned around not to be seen
For frighten kids I think would she
The beast, she had her eye on me

Escape I must, and quickly go
'Twas not to be, I was too slow
She'd snuck up on me from behind
Grabbed my hips and began to grind
I broke her grip and spun around
My actions met by quite a frown
I pushed her back and grabbed my beer
Threw it back, "I'm out of here"
"But wait," she said as I did flee
She couldn't move as fast as me
Thankfully

STRANGELY ESTRANGED

Estranged from his wife
A cheater caught twice
She'd nothing to say
Her husband was gay
How could he have done
Some guy in the bum?
She felt so betrayed
How could he have strayed?
And left her behind
For some guy's behind
To hell he will go?
She'd sure like to know
She wants him to pay
The stray that went gay

THE WATER OF LIFE

The water of life
The civilized drink
A whisky from Fife
Or was it Elgin

No matter it does
We'll just try them all
A bad idea it was
They covered the wall

So many there are
We shouldn't have tried
That night at the bar
Someone could have died

The next morning was rough
Many drinks did we have
We weren't feeling so tough
A solution we did have

For there's no better cure
Than the water of life
And of this I am sure
Breakfast whisky in Fife

THE MORNING SALUTE

You rise to attention
At first glimpse of the sun
You proudly salute me
For a long night of fun

I walk to the bathroom
My friend is impressed
Her gaze doesn't leave me
Glad I'm still undressed

Still raring to go
What a good little soldier
I climb back in the sack
And I roll my friend over

My actions are met
By a serious smile
My soldier takes over
For the next little while

He aims to impress
Oh what else can I say
The lady feels blessed
For a crazy good lay

ALL I WANT IS YOU

Just the thought of you
Just the sight of you
Just the feel of you
Just the touch of you
Just the taste of you
Just to be with you
Just to be in you
I want all of you

SUMMER LOVING

Sitting on the edge of a dock
Feet splashed into calm waters
The cool lake water refreshes
A scorching day made bearable
Relaxation sets in
A beer in hand and stress is gone
Days don't get much better

Off to the side a splash is made
Gazing over, nothing is seen
Not until she immerges from the lake
Scaling the small ladder
Each step almost in slow motion
Water dripping from her body
She climbs onto the dock
Water falling off her naked body
She stood there, looking my way
The sun glistening off her perfect skin
Silently she motions for me to come join her
Off with my shorts
The day just got better

BEAUTIFUL BUSHES

Woman are like beautiful roses
Stunning, striking, magnificent
Sweet smelling with velvet skin
Very pleasing on the eyes
With lots of little barbs in between
Ready to prick you on a whim

DISGRACEFUL

Tomorrow, tomorrow
I'll pay you tomorrow
For services rendered
Illegally tendered

I will thank you today
And tomorrow I'll pay
He had said to her face
That man's a disgrace

Those ladies work hard
Without any regard
So don't try to screw them
Just pay them then screw them

OUT WITH THE OLD

Like an arrow to the heart
It was pain without refrain
I loved it from the start
What did you have to gain?

That t-shirt was my favorite
I got it ten years past
So what if holes were in it
I could have made it last

From my closet it was pillaged
Had been washed a thousand times
You discarded it like garbage
To me that is a crime

No I don't want a new shirt
The old one was just fine
Your decision has made me hurt
For that t-shirt was mine

ONE MAN'S TRASH IS ANOTHER MAN'S TREASURE

A sight to behold
So brash and so bold
A beauty was she
With mean temper streak
No loving embrace
A drink in his face
He'd had quite enough
She strutted her stuff
He went to go leave
Wiped his face with sleeve
And never looked back
She couldn't react
The moral is old
And this is it told
No matter how hot
A lady is thought
To be, there's a man
Who can no more stand
To put up with her
For any longer

HEY BABY

Hey there sexy lady
Why don't you come over here
I've got something I'd like to share with you
It surely won't disappoint
But first how about a cocktail
Or may I suggest the gin
What? No, I've never heard that before
Panty remover? I swear I didn't know
But it does sound fun doesn't it
Maybe you should give it a try
Come on baby, don't be shy
I don't bite, hard that is

FILTHY ROTTEN

Syphilis and Gonorrhea are just words
Don't let them control your life
But if you do have them
Please get some drugs
Don't spread that around

Because they may just be words
But they are dirty words my friend
They make things burn and sting
And I mean things that shouldn't burn
Or that should only burn with passion

BLOW THAT MOTHER DOWN

It's a long way to the top
If you start from the bottom
But if you blow that mother down
Then it ain't so far at all

MEDITERRANEAN SUMMER

Sitting in the shade
On a hot summer's day
Subtle breeze blowing over me
I can't help but think how lucky I am
To be in the South of Spain
On a Mediterranean beach
For there are plenty of young beautiful women here
And bikini tops are not in fashion this year
Yippy cay yay

BAKER'S DOZEN

Why is a baker's dozen thirteen?
Why isn't it the same dozen that everyone else uses?
Is it because bakers are just more generous than others?
I put the theory to the test
I went to the bakery and asked for a dozen cookies
You know how many I got?
I got twelve, not thirteen
I was pissed
I really thought I was going to get thirteen
After throwing a bit of a fit I left
That puts that theory to rest

TAKE THE HINT

Many nights have come and gone
But there's no end in sight
You call me every single day
So far I've been polite

I've told you but a dozen times
To kindly leave me be
We had our wild and crazy night
And now I've set you free

Our time was like a blossomed rose
Magnificent indeed
But short the life that it doth have
Not long can it succeed
It's time for you to take the hint
And forget about me
Although I'm sure that's hard to do
Since I'm so damn sexy

WHAT DID YOU SAY?

If I was right and you were wrong
Would that mean that I heard you wrong?
Would wars begin and worlds collide?
Should I just take it all in stride?

A woman I thought capable not
Of uttering a contrite thought
This is a first I have to say
For seldom have I got my way

So if this happens to you men
And you would like it time again
Don't gloat or brag or rub it in
You'll find you're never right again

ODE TO WHISKY

Oh to whisky
The water of life
Where would I be
Were you not in my life

My swayed drunken values
My clouded judgments
You've caused many bruises
And crazy incidents

But you make life exciting
The dullness escapes
Your gift keeps on giving
Through great escapades

Ladies can't resist
That sweet whisky charm
I lay it on thick
For what is the harm?

YACHT LIFE

I wish that I were wealthy
I wish I had a yacht
Cause I've learned from the movies
That women love a yacht

If rap videos mean anything
Then yachts are where it's at
The ladies sunbath in the nude
And some dance in your lap

You rub them down with lotion
They rub each other too
Then feed them gin martinis
Their bottoms will undo

GIRL'S NIGHT

Girl's night at a friend's house
Several ladies in a room
All dressed in nice pajamas
A movie on the tube

They're gabbing and they're giggling
A popcorn piece is thrown
A pillow fight gets on its way
The ladies are getting warm

Their clothing being downsized
A lot of skin now showing
The pillow fighting takes a turn
And now there is some kissing

Two women going at it
The others sit and watch
It's getting hot and heavy
She's going for her crotch

I've been told this isn't accurate
Of lady's nights you see
But this is what I speculate
For I'm not there to see

THE PSYCHE OF A WOMAN

How are men to understand
The psyche of a woman
When woman do not understand
The psyche of a woman

Just ask a lady what she wants
And there will be no answer
For she does not know what she wants
How could there be an answer?

A woman comes to you with problems
But they don't want solutions
They just want to talk about their problems
And not hear your solutions

I've found that to figure women out
Is an impossible of tasks
Don't try to figure women out
Forget about that task

Just realize that you're always wrong
And that she is always right
For even if you aren't wrong
My friend she is still right

THE FAST LANE

Living life in the fast lane
Loving it 'cause it's insane
Banging ladies two at a time
All of it on the publisher's dime

Ok, that is all a lie
I get a little piece of a little pie
But I think it would be crazy
If the ladies would all go crazy
For a sexy bitch of a poet
Like Matty Cox, you know it

So come on ladies scream my name
For I want fortune and the fame
But fortune alone would suffice
Enough to treat you ladies nice

THE WORLD'S OLDEST PROFESSION?

How do we know the world's oldest profession
Was not construction or the practice of medicine
Why do we assume it to be prostitution
How did this truth ever come to fruition
For is money not needed to complete the transaction
To purchase a lady to get you some action
You'd have to have worked a previous job
Or perhaps you would just have had to rob
But either way you'd have to pay
And for that you'd have to have worked a day

IF THIS VAN'S A ROCKIN'

Loving in the back seat of a car
Parked off a dark road by the bar
The vehicle's windows steaming up
Awkwardly she climbs on top

The car it starts to rock and sway
A seatbelt's kind of in the way
You lift to throw it to the side
She bangs her head while in mid-stride

She says that she is still ok
You get back to it and on your way
No stopping now, you've gone so far
Two love crossed drunkards from the bar

VAIN

I think that I will never see
A lady as lovely as me
Nor such a man I understand
For my ego is very grand

My locks doth flow
And my eyes doth glow
My muscles ripple like the sea
Other men wish they were me

Ladies want me constantly
To fight them off I'd have to flee
But why would I do such a thing
Toss them like rubbish to the bin

That would not be my style at all
That is because I want them all
I think that I will never see
A lady who longs not for me

THANK YOU

A better man I could not be
Because of your help sculpting me
To be the man I am today
Thank you Mom on Mother's Day

You raised me in a Vegas lounge
And backstage in the showgirl lounge
You helped to teach me right from wrong
At night you'd sing to me a song

I learned from you that life is crazy
And that you always treat a lady
With the utmost of respect
Even women who are wrecked

And now that I am grown and raised
I have nothing but highest praise
For all the women who adore me
And who take their clothes off for me

DIDN'T SEE THAT COMING

Making love in a grassy field
Soft blanket beneath us
Sun warming my bare back
Nothing around us for acres

It feels so perfect
At one with each other
At one with nature
Or so I thought

A bird flew overhead
Chirping, it dropped a deuce
Splat, directly on my back
I didn't see that coming

MAN NAMED SUE

There once was a man named Sue
Who quite liked a woman named Lou
He went to her house
Unbuttoned her blouse
And told Lou he wanted to screw

THE STORK

There once was a boy from New York
Who thought babies came from the stork
Then he caught his Mom
On top of a John
Who was giving her quite a good pork

VEGAS BABY

There was once a boy raised in Vegas
Who's mother made money off her ass
He got schooled at the bar
It took him quite far
Now he gets all the ass in Vegas

THE GROTTO

I once knew a guy named Stan
Who was a big Playboy Fan
We snuck into the Grotto
By driving his auto
Fast past the giant doorman

BAMBI

There once was a woman named Bambi
Who'd make all the patron's quite randy
She'd dance on the stage
They'd rant and they'd rave
When Bambi would tear off her panties

FATE?

Blades of sand
Blowing down the beach
A sign perhaps
Calling to me

Following its lead
I walk a mile
Around a bend I go
In front of my eyes
A glorious sight
A nude photo shoot

Waves crashing the shoreline
Crashing where she lay
Splashing her naked flesh
Water dripping from her breasts
I stand in awe
In total amazement
What a lucky man I am

CLEAVAGE

You've caused eyes to bulge and men to stare
But look too long and get a glare
Most likely from your loving wife
But that is all just part of life

For why on Earth would she be wearing
Something that is just so daring
Her breasts are popping from her dress
If they fell out that'd be the best

If she would sneeze that just might happen
The men would have a pleased reaction
You've got to love the push-up bra
That garment deserves a hurrah

PIONEERS OF LOVE

Grab your moon boots baby
We're going for a ride
I'm going to make love to you
High up in the sky
Where gravity does not exist
Who's on top and who's on bottom?
Hey there goes the bed
Sex in space is craziness
It's going to blow your mind
I'm pretty sure it's never been done
That makes us pioneers
Pioneers of love

LOOKING FOR LOVE

Looking for love in an empty bottle
Coming up short every night
The drink should not be to drown your sorrow
The drink is but a lubricant
To loosen her up and make her judgment
A little shy and a wee bit clouded
At least if you are not too handsome
I have no problem in the handsome department
My presence is like panty remover
So maybe you should drown your sorrows
And I hope that you will find love
At the bottom of that empty bottle

IT'S A DOG

A princess from birth
Totted in your big purse
Your little toy puppy
You silly old yuppie

Put your dog down
Put it right on the ground
It has legs for a reason
It doesn't matter the season

You will not let it walk
All it can do is talk
It just yaps all the day
For you won't let it play

It's a dog, not a toy
And he's a frickin boy
So take that pink bow
Off of his little fro
You thin little crazy
Demented old lady

SOLDIER OF LOVE

I'm a soldier of love
In a world of despair
Sent to spread my free love
Through the world everywhere

When I'm asked what's my type
I don't know what to say
All women are my type
That's the same everyday

I don't discriminate
That is not my way
I just want to fornicate
Give and get a good lay

I'm a soldier of love
If you get in my path
We will make some sweet love
It's an awesome warpath

DEEPNESS

The world is so lonely
If you're all alone
That is some deep poetry
To write on my own

I'm a modern day guy
Who philosophizes
Don't get that in your eye
If it gushes and guises

I've lost my train of thought
For my mind's in the gutter
Surely can I focus not
I want to dip you in butter

LAZY FRIDAY

All alone on a Friday's eve
No one around for a relieve
So then I reach out for the phone
For I am feeling quite alone

I need a woman to appease me
Preferably one who is quite sleazy
It's been a long hard week at work
I've got no energy to flirt

Or to drive out to the bar
Tonight it's feeling pretty far
So a woman I shall phone
To come on over here and bone
She needs to make a living too
It's a good thing I want to screw

SELF ESTEEM IS OVERRATED

Where would we be in this wonderful world
Were there no college girls with loose morals
The kind who may suffer from low self esteem
Who when drunk near a camera are quickly obscene

The girls who at first may appear to be shy
But give them a drink and just show them a guy
They'll start grinding and stripping, competing you see
For they need attention to boost self esteem

They pose in the mags and they strip in the bars
That great education has taken them far
But where would we be were they not in this world
I don't want to know because I love these girls

A WOMAN'S TOUCH

There's nothing like a woman's touch
Her subtle soft skin and delicateness
Especially when that tender skin
Is laying underneath of mine

Or when her soft hand is gripped around
My most prized of possessions
There's nothing like a woman's touch
That's why I cannot get enough

ROAD TRIP

Remember that day
When we were driving away
On a long drive down south
You put me in your mouth

And you took it quite far
I almost crashed my car
You risked life and limb
And even bruised your shin

That shows your dedication
You have my appreciation
You're a woman of class
And you have a great ass

SUMMER SCENERY

Summer time is drawing near
Time for sun and time for beer
But most importantly of all
It's time for babes to bear it all

For when the sun is running hot
The ladies like to ditch the cloth
Booty shorts and bikini tops
Excess cleavage and flip flops

Summer brings us many gifts
Bikini babes must be the best
That's what summer means to me
It's all about the scenery

COUGAR SIGHTING

Stalking her prey from in the bar
She saw him drive up in his car
Old enough to be his mother
That sort of thing for her's no bother

She quite prefers it anyways
Says younger men are better lays
Waits 'til he's nye and then she pounces
After she's downed several ounces

Drinks the cheapest booze in house
And after she's undone her blouse
Moment's later she's drawn near
He's overcome with sudden fear

No chance he stands now in her sights
He cannot put up a good fight
Against a cougar such as her
She's even donned herself in fur

She quickly throws herself upon him
And latches on to one of his limbs
He figures there is no escape
If she were a man this would be rape

To all you cougars at the bar
Roar

LOVING IN AN ELEVATOR

Stuck inside an elevator
No way to escape
It's been down awhile already
Help is on the way
Trapped beside a beautiful woman
I can't believe my luck
If I'm to be stuck here for some time
No better company could I have
We start to talk, I work my charm
I have her eating from my palm
It begins to get quite warm
There is no air circulation at all
I take off my shirt to cool
Soon she does the same
She moves closer to me
Now we're almost touching
Body language never lies
She wants me now and I know it
"It sure is hot" I say to her
"Why don't I help you out of those"
She nodded a please and took my hand
And we made love right then and there
A few minutes later we were rescued
Bitter sweet it was
I never even got her name
But the memory will last for ever

WOMEN ARE LIKE RAINBOWS

Women are like the rainbow
So many differences to bestow
Some are big and some are small
Some are fat and others tall

Some play hard to get at times
Others have naughty pastimes
Some like to play innocent
Others to all things consent

But there is one thing shared by all
That is I want to shag them all
I guess that I should specify
Only ones easy on the eye

MEN ARE FROM MARS

If men are from Mars and women from Venus
We came to the planet that was in between us
Mars I am sure would have been very lawless
Venus itself would have been rather flawless

So why would the women have fled such a place
Those actions would not have been made with haste
There is only one idea I can harness
They obviously were in search of the penis

MOTHER NATURE'S MEDICINE

If lonely nights do need some vigour
Open up a bottle of liquor
It's mother nature's medicine
But it could become a toxin

If you partake of it too much
So just relax and take a touch
If inexperienced you are
The feeling may be quite bizarre

Go get a lady in your car
And bring her back to your boudoir
Your lonely night has fast become
An evening that is full of fun

UNFAITHFULLY BURIED

Unhappily married
Unfaithfully buried
Mistakes he had made
And for them he paid

His wife caught him cheating
And while he was sleeping
He met his demise
His wife she was wise

She dragged him out back
Inside of a sack
A hole she had made
In it now he laid

In his shallow plot
With tree right on top
No more will he be
Unfaithful to she

SEXY THREADS

They come in many different fashions
All depending on your passions
Some of them may be concealing
Other ones are quite revealing

Some of them are red and lacy
Most of them are pretty sexy
Many men don't have a preference
But I'm not one to sit on the fence

My favorite panties I have to say
Are ones that I have peeled away
From your sexy little body
Just as we are getting naughty

TO THE TOP

I have always dreamed of working a job
Where I could sleep my way to the top
Not through work or dedication
But merely lots of copulation

Could I increase my salary
And have a job where I am free
To delegate away my work
So that I'm always free to flirt

And have my way with all the interns
Or any one who works for the firm
A dream job that would surely be
I fear they exist but on TV

DIRTY BLONDE

I saw her sitting across the lobby
Long blonde hair, low cut dress
She noticed me noticing her
I could tell that she liked to be noticed

I walked to the bar and got two drinks
Then I made my way over to her
"Compliments of the bartender," I said
"More like compliments of you," she replied

I smiled a sly smile and she did the same
I asked for her name and she asked mine
Sitting beside her I passed her the drink

"This doesn't buy your way to my room," she said
"You've got me pegged all wrong," I said in reply
"We're going back to my room instead," I said
She just smiled and took a sip

"Dirty gin martini," she said, "how did you know?"
"I figured anything dirty would probably do"
"I'll show you dirty," she said
Then she dragged me back to her room

LADY OF THE NIGHT

A lady of the night
She was quite a delight
You for sure could not say
She did not earn her pay

Wine and dine her in style
She'll go the extra mile
When you take her back to
The hotel room with you

A BEAUTY LIKE NO OTHER

To me there is no greater beauty
Than a woman who is truly
Devoted to the happiness
Of men like me, I must attest

Selflessly puts her needs aside
And to your needs she does abide
A woman such as her you see
Will fulfill every fantasy

So raise your glass and toast her high
She always gives it such a try
A beauty like no other beauty
Full of lust and love and duty

JUNGLE WARFARE

It's a jungle out there
If you weren't aware
Full of fierce predators
That can lurk everywhere

So for your own protection
Always pack contraception
For you never know when
You may get some action

DISGRACEFUL

Illegitimate race
A fall from grace
Fixing ballots
By opening wallets

Look what you've done
You have become
A laughing stock
From once good stock

Go run and hide
For you don't abide
By the rules of the race
Now you are a disgrace

A LITTLE TIPSY

Unable to focus
Or walk a straight line
Perhaps that's enough
Of the old cellar wine

Oh, why not another?
I slur as I speak
It surely can't hurt
To have one more squeak

I pour us another
And upstairs I go
I swagger and stagger
And over I go

Tumbling down the stairs
Loose from all of the wine
I don't hurt a thing
And arise feeling fine

Perhaps that's a sign
I think to myself
All this wine it appears
Can be good for my health

MAN WHORE

Business dealings by phone
Then he goes to their home
Takes them out on the town
Never does leave a frown

A man whore by trade
That is how he gets paid
Business is really good
For they all love his wood

And he treats them quite nice
Just like sugar and spice
To make the ladies pay
For a really good lay

POLITICALLY CORRECT

Political correctness
Is bringing this world down
Everyone is so sensitive
In vomit I could drown

All this crap it gags me
You can't say this or that
If someone is a mammoth whale
Why can't I call them fat?

A white man I will call you
If pasty white your skin
And black is what I'll call you
If you have melanin

No beating 'round the bushes
And walking on eggshells
Only a fool does act this way
Free speech he hopes to quell

Throw PC out the window
Bury her in the ditch
And sprout a sack there nancy boy
Stop being such a bitch

FREE RIDE

Some women will marry a man for his money
Some women are groupies, others puck bunnies
But are there no men that do these kind of things?
Would men degrade themselves just for some bling?

I'm sure some men would if they could find a way
And one of those ways is to become a gay
And find an old queen who just wants to be seen
With a young handsome man who is barely nineteen

WINTER LOVING

The ground is disguised in a white blanket of snow
We are covered by a white blanket of down
Winter loving beneath the covers

It is heating up and I'm getting sweaty
I throw the blankets to the side
You pull them right back over us

How can I be so warm and you so cold?
We both are lying in the same bed
It's like an August day under these covers

Slowly this time I inch away the sheets
Somehow you still seem to notice
Like a little chess match we now have going

So I kick it up a notch, the loving that is
The blankets fall off now but your mind is elsewhere
You are finally too distracted to notice

I've won the battle of the blanket
But now that does not really matter
For we are both about to win

TIRE BITERS

He bought it strictly
To get with the ladies
His shiny red car
He hoped would take him far

He pulls up to a club
Gives the hood a good rub
Some ladies take notice
He's hoping for coitus

Many ladies you know
Cannot let a man go
Who they think has money
They will act quite slutty

To get his attention
They'll pay him affection
And hope that in turn
They can go for a burn

With him in his car
Be seen leaving the bar
With someone with money
It's really quite funny

The ladies you see
Who cannot let a man be
That has a nice car
Tire biters they are

But he doesn't care
He wants people to stare
Under his breath he mutters
I love tire biters

THE METER MAID

It seems to me
That life would be
So much improved
Were you removed

A minute late
Infuriate
A ticket left
You are bereft

Of compassion
Provocation
You do not need
To do your deed

You get your joy
When you annoy
Society
With your duty

SCREW THE LIFE SENTENCE

Living in a prison
Searching for my freedom
The man has got me down

I cannot break the shackles
Though try and try I do
This existence seems so futile

Punch in Monday morning
Punch out Friday eve
Then two days left for living

No longer can I take this
Life is too short too suffer
Through pointless monotony

Escape I must, a plan I need
To break these chains and get away
I must accomplish something with my life

A book of awesome poems
Is what I plan on writing
To blow everybody's minds

Look out World for here I come
On the loose and on the run
I'm going to put my poems in you all

A TRUE GENTLEMAN

I want to love you
And her also
That girl over there too
I want to love you all

Come back to my place
It'll just be the four of us
We'll make love through the night
Then come morning you can all leave

I'll promise to call you
But that call will never come
Lucky for you though
You'll always have that night to remember

BIG CHANGES

We used to date
But we broke up
And then one day
She looked me up

She wrote to say
She'd like to meet
Excited I
Was for the greet

How she had changed
Not subtly
For now she had
A large pee pee

A man she was
So shocked was I
Surgically changed
She was a guy

I did not know
How to react
Her vage was gone
She had a sack

Frightened at first
But calmed did I
My old girlfriend
Was now a guy

BLOWING BUBBLES

Pina Coladas
Down by the pool
The sun is shinning
Damn this is cool

Surrounded by gorgeous
And some topless women
This must be what it's like
Way up in heaven

I hop in the pool
Without spilling my drink
I look to a lady
And give her a wink

She dives in the pool
And swims up beside me
I give her my drink
She puts her hand on me

Before I know it
My shorts she has off
She takes a breath in
And goes down for liftoff

People surrounding
But no one can see
This beautiful woman
Has gone down on me

CHAIN GANG

Working on a chain gang
On a lonesome highway
Paying off my dept
For crimes that hurt no one

Why is it illegal
To operate a brothel
I don't understand it
Politicians are my clients

SHOWER SCENE

It's early in the morning
The air has quite a chill
She wishes she was snoring
But has to pay the bills

She steps inside the shower
The water's running hot
She's getting a good lather
Her body's smoking hot

The mirror's getting steamy
As she rubs her body down
She's very slick and soapy
From her little rubdown

There would be nothing better
Than to climb in there too
And take her in the shower
Just like a love guru

THE FRIENDLY HITCHHIKER

Riding down the highway
Warm breeze in my face
The bike's engine revving beneath me
Her arms wrapped tight around my chest

Her grip loosens slightly
Hands sliding down my front
Nudging my zipper open
Moments later we have liftoff

I roll back on the throttle
Keeping my mind on the road
Her mind appears to be elsewhere
This chick's really something

First hitchhiker I've ever picked up
And I'm sure glad I did
A good tug while I'm riding
That was a first, even for me

BROKEN FILTER

I say inappropriate things
At inappropriate times
Some people have a filter
What happened to mine?

When people are all a whisper
Like at an art gallery
My whispering caries
To spread my profanity

I get dirty looks
For spreading my humour
It is not my fault
These people are bitter

That I have the guts
To call a spade a spade
If a piece of art sucks
I'll say throw it away

Maybe my filter's fine
It's the rest that are broken
My inappropriateness
Is but my comic weapon

TOO SEXY

Is it possible to be too sexy?
I think that it is not
A woman said that to me once
And she was very hot

She said that men were nervous around her
Because she was so beautiful
I said that it most likely was
Those men's skills were quite pitiful

So I pulled out the sexy talk
And she began to melt
I gently brushed hair from her face
Then she went for my belt

If too sexy she be for other men
She'd finally met her match
I carried her up to my room
We both had an itch to scratch

FASHION SHOW

Why is it when going out
On the town for an evening
Before you can leave from the house
Your lady has a routine

She has to try on everything
She owns without exception
And if a comment you do make
My man you may be beaten

You wonder why she has to wait
Until the last of minutes
To sample everything she owns
And empty out her closets

And in the end what does she wear
But the first thing she tried
Now late you are to meet your friends
But mention it and die

SPEEDOS

Speedos are a funny thing
They're tight and hold your package in
On fat guys ladies love them not
On fit men ladies think they're hot

When on a European beach
The Speedo look is what they preach
But here in North America
The Speedo's far from the alpha

I like to pull the Speedos out
When there are ladies all about
To draw their attention to me
I strut my stuff quite shamelessly

COCK BLOCKED (UNINTENTIONALLY)

I called my bud the other day
To drop a line and just say "hey"
He answered after the fourth ring
Preoccupied, turns out he'd been

He was starting to get busy
With his lovely little lady
Instead of letting his phone ring
He picked it up, oh what a sin

For it is written in the code
When business time at the abode
Don't put your gorgeous babe on hold
Or you may never lose your load

Your bud will always understand
That business time trumps man to man
So let that phone ring off the hook
If your lady gives you that look

THE DEGENERATE FAMILY

At the ocean on a summer's day
Warm breeze blowing through your hair
Sun shining in the clear blue sky
Waves gently crashing upon the beach
A kite flies high up in the sky
The warm sand wraps around your feet
You feel your stress all melt away
And now you're finally at peace

From out of nowhere they appear
With screaming children for all to hear
They trample by without regard
While kicking sand upon your face
Your blood begins to slowly boil
The peaceful day is all but gone
The day's beauty overshadowed now
By the inconsiderate degenerate family

The terrors to the water go
Perhaps, you think, they might just drown
The world would surely miss them none
From out of the air, seagulls appear
They circle round, wings spread wide
And what doth fall but from the rear
But quite a large specimen
The excrement contacts the head
Of one of the rotten children
And splashes all across his face

Oh this was Karma at work today
The child begins to whale quite loud
To the chagrin of all the crowd
They have no choice but for to leave
The little terror will not calm down
Goodbye you trash we'll miss you none
Your stress once again fades away
Oh what a beautiful day this is

NO ACCOUNTABILITY

The world has gone mad
Our laws have gone bad
We cannot succeed
We're run by inbreeds

Or is it just me
Have I gone crazy
The lines have been blurred
This world is absurd

A revolution
I have just begun
I'll take to the street
These fools we'll defeat

They run us straight down
Right into the ground
Our politicians
Are mostly cretins

Their expense accounts
Easily surmounts
The incomes of most
Of which they do boast

They hide all their books
These people are crooks
Things need to be changed
For they are deranged

But what can we do
To this reckless crew
Let's throw them in jail
Without any bail

I'LL HAIKU YOU IN THE FACE

Shenanigans

Hotel room
Shenanigans
It all stays here

Women's Rights

Escort Service
Well paid ladies
Praise women's lib

Plunging Neck Lines

Loose fitting blouse
Bending over
Showing the goods

Paid to Leave

Rented by the hour
No time to shower
Leave

Legalized

Red light district
No crime committed
It's legal here

Misunderstanding

I'll haiku you in the face
She pulled mace
Crazy bitch

Slurred Words

At the bar
Crushing hard
Take me drunk I'm home

The main text of this book is set in BEMBO, a typeface family designed by Stanley Morison in 1929. It was based on a typeface designed by Francesco Griffo, who worked as a punch-cutter for famed early printer and publisher Aldus Manutius in Venice. The typeface was first used in February 1496, in the setting of a 60 page text written by the young Italian humanist poet Pietro Bembo, later a Cardinal and secretary to Pope Leo X.

The title page is set in **CHAMPION GOTHIC MIDDLEWEIGHT**, a typeface family designed by Jonathan Hoefler in 1990. Originally developed for *Sports Illustrated*, the Champion Gothic series was created to help designers deal with headlines of different lengths. American woodtypes of the late nineteenth century served as the inspiration for Champion Gothic, in both form and philosophy.

DON'T BE A DOUCHEBAG
A MAN'S GUIDE TO ETIQUETTE

What happens when the ultimate man writes the ultimate book? Matthew James doesn't know either. But he is a man, and he did write this book.

Don't Be A Douchebag: A Man's Guide To Etiquette is more than just a mere book. It is a tool that can be used to smoothly guide you through life's bumpy journey. The book can teach, it can preach, and it can literally raise your children better than you can, figuratively speaking.

Laugh, cry, and quite possibly reach potentially hazardous blood pressure levels as you navigate your way through the pages of this well-crafted masterwork. Full of strong opinions, comedic rants and anecdotes, you will be hard pressed to put down this book once you are hit with uncontrollable laughter.

A self-proclaimed "real man's" attempt to put the word man back into man, Matthew James has crafted a hilarious, if not irrelevant, book for the modern man. Not for the faint of heart or over-protective mothers, *Don't be a Douchebag* is an instant classic, sure to entertain from cover to cover.

Don't Be A DOUCHEBAG

A Man's Guide to Etiquette

Matthew James

MATHEW JAMES FOR PRESIDENT LOOK OUT, AMERICA!

That's right, America! You never asked for it and you were heard, loud and clear. Matthew James is a man possessed. You can sleep with one eye open. You can sleep with the other one open too. But it won't matter because nothing is going to prevent Matthew James from becoming the next president of the United States of America.

With rugged good looks, an IQ that is boldly average and a Canadian passport, Matthew James is more than equipped to lead the American people wherever they need to be lead. His platforms on such topics as war, the economy and national security will revolutionize the world, and when Matthew speaks of the world, he means America.

Matthew James is a man of the people. Matthew James is a man who is people. Matthew James is a leader of the people. Matthew James will, in 2016, be the commander in chief of the American people.

His political manifesto will gently assault your soul. Read it, fall in love with it, and fall in love with your next president, America. This political manifesto will change your life, perhaps even for the better. Do yourself the best thing you've ever done in the past minute of your life and read this book. America! America! America?

Matthew James for PRESIDENT

Look out, America!

www.ingramcontent.com/pod-product-compliance
Ingram Content Group UK Ltd.
Pitfield, Milton Keynes, MK11 3LW, UK
UKHW041828200726
13854UKWH00002BA/873

9 781772 260113